OBATALA

IFÁ AND THE SPIRIT OF THE CHIEF OF THE WHITE CLOTH

AWO FÁ'LOKUN FATUNMBI
OMO AWO FATUNMISE, ILE IFE,
BABALAWO ÈGBÈ IFÁ, ODE REMO,
OLÚWO ILÉ ÒRÚNMÌLÀ OSHUN, OAKLAND, CA

OBATALA; Ifa and the Spirit of the White Cloth
By Awo Fa'lokun Fatunmbi

Original Publications
P.O. Box 236
Old Bethpage, New York 11804-0236
(888) OCCULT-1

www.OCCULT1.com

Printed in the United States of America

ACKNOWLEDGEMENTS

The material in this book is primarily based on oral instruction from the elders of *Ifá* in Ode Remo, Ogun State, Nigeria and Ile Ife, Oshun State, Nigeria. In appreciation for their time, patience and loving concern for my training and spiritual guidance I say: *A dúpé Ègbè Ifá Ode Remo, Babalawo* Adesanya Awoyade, *Babalawo* Babalola Akinsanya, *Babalawo* Saibu Lamiyo, *Babalawo* Odujosi Awoyade, *Babalawo* Olu Taylor, *Babalawo* Abokede Aralbadan, *Babalawo* Biodun Debona, *Babalawo* Oluwasina Kuti, *Babalawo* Afolabi Kuti, *Babalawo* Fagbemi Fasina, *Babalawo* Oropotoniyan and all the members of *Ègbè Apetebi Ode Remo*.

Additional material in this book is based on instruction from the elders of Ile Ife, Oshun State, Nigeria. In appreciation to them I say: *A dúpé Awon Ifá Fatunmise Ègbè Ifá Ilé Ife, Jolofinpe* Falaju Fatunmise, *Babalawo* Ganiyu Olaifa Fatunmise, *Babalawo* Awoleke Awofisan Lokore, *Babalawo* Ifaioye Fatunmise, *Babalawo* Ifanimowu Fatunmise, *Babalawo* Ifasure Fatunmise, *Babalawo* Adebolu Fatunmise and all the members of *Ègbè Apetebi Awon Fatunmise*.

A special thank you to the members of *Ilé Òrúnmìlà Oshun* for their continuing support and understanding: *Olori Yeye Awor Timi Lade, Apetebi Orunmila, Iya l'Orisha Oshun Miwa* (Luisah Teish), *Eko'fa Iya l'Orisha Omijinka, Iya l'Orisha Iya Oshun Iya Osogbo, Iya l'Orisha Shango Wenwa*, Leona Jacobs-White, Nzinga Denny, Earthea Nance, Vance Williams, Blackberri, Salim Abdul-Jelani, Rebecca Schiros, Carol Lanigan, Zena Attig, T'hisha, Rose Schadt, Xochipala Maes Valdez, Dee Orr, Nina Heft, Ishoke, Luis Mangual and Earl White. A grateful thanks to *Awo Medahoci* and *Iya Omolade*.

A final thank you to Maureen Pattarelli for her work in editing this manuscript. *Orunmila a buru, a boye, a bosise.*

Awo Fá'lokun Fatunmbi

TABLE OF CONTENTS

INTRODUCTION

Obatala is the Spirit of the Chief of White Cloth in the West African religious tradition called *"Ifá."* The word *Obatala* is the name given to describe a complex convergence of Spiritual Forces that are key elements in the *Ifá* concept of consciousness. Those Spiritual Forces that form the foundation of *Obatala's* role in the Spirit Realm relate to the movement between dynamics and form as it exists throughout the universe. According to *Ifá*, dynamics and form represent the polarity between the Forces of expansion and contraction. Together these Forces create light and darkness, which in turn sustains and defines all that is. *Ifá* teaches that it is the interaction between light and darkness that generates the physical universe, and it is *Obatala* who brings this interaction into Being.

There is no literal translation for the word *Ifá*. It refers to a religious tradition, an understanding of ethics, a process of spiritual transformation and a set of scriptures that are the basis for a complex system of divination.

Ifá is found throughout the African diaspora where it spread as an integral part of Yoruba culture. The Yoruba Nation is located in the southwestern region of Nigeria. Prior to colonization, the Yoruba Nation was a federation of city-states that was originally centered in the city of *Ilé Ifę̀*. According to *Ifá* myth, the Yorubas migrated to *Ilé Ifę̀* from the east under the leadership of a warrior chief named *Oduduwa*. It is difficult to date the time of the Yoruba move into West Africa because of limited archaeological research on the subject. Estimates range from between sixteen hundred to twenty-five hundred years ago. It is likely that migration took place over a number of generations. As the population grew, each new city-state that became a part of the Yoruba federation was governed by a chief called *"Oba."* The position of *Oba* is a form of hereditary monarchy and each *Oba* goes through an initiation that makes them a spiritual descendant of *Oduduwa*

Traditional Yoruba political institutions are very much integrated with traditional Yoruba religious institutions. Both structures survived British rule in Nigeria, and continue to function alongside the current civil government.

Within the discipline of *Ifá*, there is a body of wisdom called "*awo*," which attempts to preserve the rituals that create direct communication with Forces in Nature. *Awo* is a Yoruba word that is usually translated to mean "secret." Unfortunately, there is no real English equivalent to the word *awo*, because the word carries strong cultural and esoteric associations. In traditional Yoruba culture, *awo* refers to the hidden principles that explain the Mystery of Creation and Evolution. *Awo* is the esoteric understanding of the invisible forces that sustain dynamics and form within Nature. The essence of these invisible forces are not considered secret because they are devious, they are secret because they remain elusive, awesome in their power to transform and not readily apparent. As such they can only be grasped through direct interaction and participation. Anything which can be known by the intellect alone ceases to be *awo*.

The primal inspiration for *awo* is the communication between transcendent Spiritual Forces and human consciousness. This communication is believed to be facilitated by the Spirit of *Eṣu*, who is the Divine Messenger. Working in close association with *Eṣu* is *Ògún*, who is the Spirit of Iron. *Ògún* has the power to clear away those obstacles that stand in the way of spiritual growth. According to *Ifá*, the work done by *Ògún* is guided by *Ochosi*, who as the Spirit of the Tracker has the ability to locate the shortest path to our spiritual goals. The essential goal that *Ochosi* is called upon to guide us towards is the task of building "*ìwà-pèlé*," which means "good character." This guidance takes the form of a spiritual quest which is called "*iwakiri*." One of the functions of *Obatala* is to preserve the Mystic Vision that to those who make the quest of *iwakiri* in search of *ìwà-pèlé*.

The power of *Obatala* is described by *Ifá* as one of many Spiritual Forces in Nature which are called "*Orisha*." The word *Orisha* means "Select Head." In a cultural context, *Orisha* is a reference to the various Forces in Nature that guide consciousness.

According to *Ifá*, everything in Nature has some form of consciousness called "*Orí*." The *Orí* of all animals, plants and humans is believed to be guided by a specific Force in Nature (*Orisha*) which defines the quality of a particular form of consciousness. There are a large number of *Orisha*, and each *Orisha* has its own *awo*.

The unique function of *Obatala* within the realm of *Orisha Awo* (Mysteries of Nature) is to provide the spark of light that animates consciousness. To call an *Orisha* the Chief of White Cloth is to make a symbolic reference to that substance which makes consciousness possible. The reference to White Cloth is not a reference to the material used to make cloth, it is a reference to the fabric which binds the universe together. The threads of this fabric are the multi-leveled layers of consciousness which *Ifá* teaches exists in all things on all levels of Being. *Ifá* teaches that it is the ability of Forces of Nature to communicate with each other, and the ability of humans to communicate with Forces in Nature that gives the world a sense of spiritual unity. It is the understanding of this ability which gives substance to the *Ifá* concept of good character, and it is *Obatala* who guides us towards developing this understanding.

Ifá teaches that all Forces in Nature come into Being through the manifestation of energy patterns called *Odu*. *Ifá* has identified and labeled 256 different *Odu* which can be thought of as different expressions of consciousness. But because consciousness itself is generated by *Obatala*, every *Odu* contains an element of *Obatala's aṣẹ* (power).

In metaphysical terms, this means that all of Creation is linked to *Obatala* as the Source of Being. *Ifá* teaches that all forms of consciousness contain a spark of *aṣẹ* (spiritual power) from *Obatala*, and it is this spark that links everything that is to its shared Beginning.

I.

ALỌ IRINTÀN OBATALA
FOLKTALES OF THE SPIRIT OF THE CHIEF
OF WHITE CLOTH

A. *OBATALA IRIN-AJO IKOLE AYE* — The Chief of White Cloth Travels to Earth

Qlọdumare (The Creator) called *Obatala* (Chief of White Cloth) to *Ikole Orun* (the Realm of the Ancestors) on the day that he wanted to create dry land on the waters of the *Ikole Aye* (Earth). *Obatala* kneeled before *Qlọdumare* and said that he did not know the *awo* (mystery) of creating land on *Ikole Aye* (Earth). *Qlọdumare* told *Obatala* that he would give him the *aşẹ* (power) to make land on *Ikole Aye* (Earth).

On the day that *Obatala* was to travel from *Ikole Orun* (The Realm of the Ancestors) to *Ikole Aye* (Earth), *Qlọdumare* gave him a *ìgbín* (snail) shell filled with earth, a five toed *ẹtù* (guinea hen), *ikin* (palm nuts) and *agẹmọ* (chameleon). *Obatala* took the *aşẹ* (power), then asked *Qlọdumare* how he was to make the journey from *Ikole Orun* (The Realm of the Ancestors) to *Ikole Aye* (Earth). *Qlọdumare* told him that he was to gather all the *iwōrò* (gold) in *Ikole Orun* (The Realm of the Ancestors) and take it to *Ògún* (The Spirit of Iron), who would forge an *ẹ̀wọn* (chain) that would link *Ikole Orun* (The Realm of the Ancestors) to *Ikole Aye* (Earth).

Ògún took all the *iwōrò* (gold) and forged a long *ẹ̀wọn* (chain), which he flung towards *Ikole Ayè* (Earth). *Obatala* placed his *aşẹ* (power) in a pouch and began the descent down the *èwòn* (chain). When he came to the last rung he could see that he was still some distance from the primal waters.

Obatala removed the *igbín* (snail) shell from his pouch and sprinkled soil upon the primal waters. Then he removed the five toed *ètù* (guinea hen) and dropped it on the land. As soon as the *ètù* (guinea hen) reached the soil it started scratching the ground, spreading dirt across the surface of the primal waters. Seeing that the ground had become firm, *Obatala* removed an *ikin* (palm nut) and dropped it on the land. The *ikin* (palm nut) sprouted and became a palm tree. When the palm tree grew to its full height, it reached the last ring of the *iwòrò 'won* (gold chain). *Obatala* was able to step from the *èwòn* (chain) to the palm tree.

After climbing down the tree, *Obatala* started to mold humans from the clay in the earth. As he worked, he became tired and decided that he needed a rest. Taking the fruit from the palm tree, he made palm wine and drank until he was ready to return to work. The humans that he molded while he was drunk did not look like the others, but *Obatala* did not notice and he kept drinking until he fell asleep.

While *Obatala* slept, *Olòdumare* gave the task of finishing Creation to *Oduduwa* (Owner of the Womb of Creation). *Olòdumare* waited for *Obatala* to awaken from his drunken sleep and told him that it was taboo for *Obatala* to taste palm wine ever again. When *Obatala* saw what had happened to the humans he had created while he was drunk, he agreed to protect all children for future generations. It was *Obatala* who said that he would never again let his White Cloth become soiled.

To this day those who worship *Obatala* say, "*Obatala o su n'nu ala, Obatala o ji n'nu ala, Obatala o tinu ala didè, Iba Obatala*," which means, "The Chief of White Cloth sleeps in white, the Chief of White Cloth awakes in white, the Chief of White cloth gets up in white, praise to the Chief of White Cloth".

Commentary: The word *Obatala* translates to mean "Chief of White Cloth." In metaphysical terms White Cloth is the primal source of the physical universe. *Ifá* teaches that light becomes transformed into darkness and that darkness becomes transformed into light. Within the unfolding of this transformation, Evolution creates greater and greater levels of complexity. The original explosion that created the universe produced massive quantities of light in the form of subatomic particles. As the universe cooled these particles joined together to form simple elements. The elements in turn joined together to form stars. In time, certain stars collapsed, forming black holes that imploded on themselves until they created a fission reaction. This sent huge clouds of complex elements throughout the universe. It was a cloud of complex elements that cooled to form the solar system, and within the solar system there evolved the ecosystems that exist on Earth.

The Myth of *Obatala* is the *Ifá* version of this sequence of events. It uses symbolic language to describe a series of evolutionary events that match closely with the theories of Creation that have been proposed by contemporary Western science. At the beginning of the Myth, *Qlǫdumare* gives *Obatala* the instruction to create the world. *Qlǫdumare* represents all potential form that exists in the universe as it remains dormant prior to manifestation. It is the White Cloth or light particles of *Obatala* that bring potential form into physical existence. Western science teaches that all of Creation evolved from the light produced during the primal explosion at the beginning of time. *Ifá* teaches that all of Creation evolved from the White Cloth of *Obatala's* robes.

The chain used by *Obatala* to travel from the Realm of the Ancestors to Earth appears to be a symbolic representation of the the structure used to transmit genetic information from one generation to the next. The genetic code that is used to form each species is passed through a biochemical substance called DNA. When DNA is viewed under a microscope it appears as a double helix, which is similar to the pattern of a chain. In *Ifá* scripture the reference to the Realm of the Ancestors includes all those Natural Forces that led to the development of human life and is not limited to human form. In Western science that DNA which exists in mammals is believed to be an extension of a chain of transmissions from single cell life forms at the bottom of the ocean to complex life forms that populate the earth.

When *Obatala* climbs down the chain towards land, he takes soil from a snail shell. The shape of the snail shell is a pattern that reccurs throughout nature. The early Greeks called this pattern the "Golden Mean." It is a series of expanding circles that get progressively larger at a steady rate. This growth pattern occurs in trees, plants, and sea life. It is the same pattern that regulates the distance of the planets from the sun. The sea shell as a sacred object associated with *Obatala* symbolizes the expansive quality of evolution.

When *Obatala* places the guinea hen on the ground, the Earth becomes a place that can support life systems. The guinea hen is sacred to *Oshun* and it has five toes, which is *Oshun's* sacred number. *Oshun* is the spirit of eroticism, fertility and abundance. At this point in the Myth, *Obatala* is introducing sexuality, reproduction and the allure of the erotic into the unfolding pattern of Creation.

In order to reach the Earth, *Obatala* plants seeds which grow into a palm tree. Within the religion of *Ifá* the palm tree is regarded as the sacred tree of life. Most earth-centered religions designate a particular tree to symbolize the transformation of all things as they progress through the cycles of birth, life, death and rebirth. When a Myth refers to a deity bringing the tree of life to Earth, it is a reference to the existence of natural laws which guide the development of ecological systems on the planet.

Obatala reaches the ground and then begins to make humans. At this point *Obatala* becomes intoxicated, and the task of finishing creation is given to *Oduduwa*. In mythic terms, this part of the Creation story suggests that the unfolding of evolution can be flawed. Defects occur in Nature and the *Ifá* Creation Myth reflects this truth. *Ifá* cosmology tends to describe the world as it is and not as it should be.

The fact that the task of Creation was taken from *Obatala* and given to *Oduduwa* appears to be a reference to the Natural Law of entropy. That law says that once an ecological system is set in motion it always moves towards inevitable extinction. By placing *Oduduwa* in charge of Creation, the myth is suggesting that there is *awo*, or mystery beyond the visible universe and beyond the

inevitability of death. *Oduduwa* is the womb of darkness through
which all rebirth emerges.

When *Obatala* agrees to keep his white cloths unsoiled, it is
a promise to continue the struggle for perfection in an flawed
universe. Without this struggle there is no existence, only primal
unity. Primal unity is described in *Ifá* scripture as the loneliness
of the Ancestors in *Ikole Orun 8888*.

B. *IJIMERE OBOTUNDE* — The Imprisonment of the Chief of White Cloth

Obatala (The Chief of White Cloth) consulted *Ifá* on the day
that he wanted to make a journey in search of *Shango* (The Spirit
of Lightning). *Ifá* said *Obatala* could only visit *Shango* after he
had learned the lessons of *irèlè* (humility). *Obatala* was confident
that he knew *awo 'rèlè* (the mystery of humility), so he made
preparations for the journey to *Oyo*.

As *Obatala* was walking down the road that led to *Oyo*, he
saw *Eşu* sitting at the crossroads. *Eşu* was about to pick up a large
calabash filled with palm oil. Seeing *Obatala's* approach, *Eşu*
asked him to help place the calabash on his head. *Obatala* reached
down and lifted the container of palm oil. When the calabash was
at chest level, *Eşu* knocked the calabash, spilling red palm oil on
Obatala's white robes.

In an effort to clean himself, *Obatala* made the journey to the
Omi Orun (The Ancestral Waters). When he reached the edge of
the river he realized that the oil had stained his vision. *Obatala*
removed his eyes from their socket and placed them on the shrine
of *Oyigiyigi* (The Stone of Creation). As he submerged himself in
the water, *Eşu* removed both eyes from the sacred rock. *Eşu* took
them to the home of *Oshun* who used *awo oyin* (the mystery of
honey) to entice them from him.

Obatala was blind on the day he started searching for his
vision. He traveled to the home of *Oshun* who said that she would
return his eyes in exchange for *awo merindinlogun* (the mystery
of cowrie shell divination). *Obatala* agreed, and from that day on
Oshun made divination available to all the *Orisha* (the Immortals).

With his eyes returned to their sockets, *Obatala* continued on his journey to *Oyo*, perplexed by the difficulties that had greeted him on his journey. Near the entrance of the city, *Obatala* saw a riderless horse charging down the road. With agility and grace, *Obatala* swung himself onto the back of the animal and brought the horse to a stop. Seeing *Obatala* on the horse, the soldiers who guarded the entrance to *Oyo* surrounded *Obatala* and accused him of being a thief. *Obatala* was thrown into prison. Inside his cell, *Obatala* contemplated *awo irèlè* (the mystery of humility).

It was on that day that the city of *Oyo* was cursed by famine, drought, infertility and disease. *Shango* consulted *Ifá* on the day that his city was on the brink of ruin. He was advised that *awo atunbi* (the mystery of regeneration) was being held in the palace prison. When *Shango* discovered *Obatala* in chains, *Shango* begged for forgiveness and offered *Obatala* everything he owned. *Obatala* greeted *Shango* and returned home without saying a word.

From that day on those who praise *Obatala* say, "*Oluwaiye rè ẹ o, ke bi owu la, o yi ala. osun l'ala, o fi koko ala rumo,*" which means "Owner of the good things in life, give me wisdom so that I may become the White Cloth, Protector of the White Cloth, I salute your power."

Commentary: Within the Cosmology of *Ifá*, *Obatala* has the function of both generating consciousness and setting the standards for ethical behavior. Given this dual role it may seem odd that *Obatala* is portrayed in this Myth as someone who misunderstands the instruction of *Ifá*, than goes through a series of crises that seem to cast doubt on his integrity. The point of presenting *Obatala* in this context is to show the potential for contradiction between intention and action.

In the Myth *Obatala* wants to visit *Shango*. This represents the very universal idea of a father wanting to meet with his son. Simply put, it is the idea of the desire to be a good parent. This is a noble idea and one that is apparently rooted in a deep respect for ethical behavior. When *Obatala* consults *Ifá*, he is told that it is not a good time to make the journey to *Oyo*. He is advised that the spiritual lesson of humility is more important than making the trip.

Being pulled by his desire for family companionship, and assuming that he understands the essence of humility, *Obatala* decides to make the trip anyway. Because his intentions are good, *Obatala* feels that he can act in opposition to the instructions from *Ifá*. This is a recurring theme throughout *Ifá* scripture and is an exploration of the relationship between self and world. What may appear to be in the best interest of the self may have the opposite effect on the world. *Ifá* teaches that our inner intentions must be in harmony with external Spiritual Forces in order for life to manifest abundance.

Part of the mystery of living in the world involves ethical choices, and another part involves doing the right thing in the right way at the right time. It is the issue of timing that *Obatala* has ignored, and because of this shortsightedness he encounters one problem after another. Those who believe that Myth should reflect life in its "ideal" state are often confused by the actions of *Orisha* in *Ifá* Myth. Here the Spirit of the Chief of White Cloth is describe in terms that make him appear incompetent and stubborn. However, *Ifá* Myth, like the Myth of most indigenous religions, uses the actions of the Spirits to give examples of those problems faced by real people who live in the real world. Stories about perfect beings living in a perfect world would be of little value to those who struggle with the real concerns of life on Earth.

Seldom does anyone deliberately do anything that they conceive of as unethical. Even people engaged in what society would call "criminal activity" have elaborate explanations that justify their actions and make them seem noble. This Myth is suggesting that living in harmony with self and world requires much more than good intentions. It requires a keen sense of those Spiritual Forces that are at play outside the self. Each time that *Obatala* encountered misfortune he had the opportunity to reevaluate his decision to make the journey to *Oyo*.

After each crisis he made the decision to continue with his travels rather than consider the importance of discovering the true meaning of humility. This decision led to more and more serious problems until the entire village of *Oyo* was adversly effected. It is at this point that *Obatala* has no other choice than to consider the lesson presented by *Ifá*. Alone, sitting in his cell, *Obatala* experiences the lesson of humility.

At the end of the Myth *Obatala* quietly returns home. This suggests that he has taken full responsibility for his actions and is reminded of the lesson of humility, which is at the core of *Ifá* ethics. In this instance the lack of humility was rooted in ignoring the warning of divination. The idea that spiritual lessons cannot be avoided when their time has come is a recurring theme in *Ifá* scripture. The choice is to face it head on or have it knock you down when you least expect it.

OBATALA, Chief of White Cloth

II.

ÌMỌ̀ OBATALA
THE THEOLOGICAL FUNCTION
OF THE SPIRIT OF THE CHIEF OF
THE WHITE CLOTH

A. OBATALA 'YÀNMÓ-ÌPIN — The Spirit of the Chief of the White Cloth and the Concept of Destiny

The *Ifá* concept of "*àyànmó-ìpin*," which means "destiny," is based on the belief that each person chooses their individual destiny before being born into the world. These choices materialize as those components that form human potential. Within the scope of each person's potential there exists parameters of choice that can enhance or inhibit the fullest expression of individual destiny. *Ifá* calls these possibilities "*òna ìpin*," which means "road of destiny." Each decision that is made in the course of one lifetime can effect the range of possibilities that exists in the future, by either limiting or expanding the options for growth.

It is within the context of choice, or what is known in Western philosophical tradition as "free will" that *Ifá* recognizes a collection of Spiritual Forces called "*Ibora*." In Yoruba, the word *Ibora* means "Warrior." Traditionally the *Ibora* include *Eṣu*, *Ògún* and *Ochosi*. *Eṣu* is the cornerstone that links the *Ibora* as they relate to the issue of spiritual growth. According to *Ifá*, each moment of existence includes a wide range of possible actions, reactions and interpretations. Those moments which require decisive action are described in *Ifá* scripture as "*ona'pade*," which means "junction in the road." Whenever a person who is trying to build character through the use of *Ifá* spiritual discipline reaches *ona'pade*, it is customary to consult *Eṣu* regarding the question of which path will bring blessings from *Orisha*.

Ifá teaches that blessings come to those who make choices that are consistent with their highest destiny. Within Yoruba culture it is understood that an individual's highest destiny is based on those choices that build "*ìwa-pèlé*," which means "good character." Those who develop good character are often described as weaving white cloth, which means creating purity and spiritual elevation in the world. The collective impact of those who weave white cloth is the entering into a state of mystical union with the Chief or the Source of White Cloth who is called *Obatala*. This is true for everyone, even those who worship other *Orisha*. *Ifá* scripture clearly suggests that all of the *Orisha* exist as an extension of the power of consciousness that is created by the *aṣẹ* (power) of *Obatala*.

For those who are initiated into *awo Obatala* (mysteries of the Chief of White Cloth) it is expected that they will take on the responsibility of setting a good example as role models in the community. Most initiates who receive the *aṣẹ* (power) of *Obatala* are given strict taboos regarding drinking, the use of foul language, the need for cleanliness and the expectation of high moral conduct. These taboos are not considered as a form of punishment. Taboos are designed to provide guidelines for the initiate as they continually search for the inner secrets of good character. Guidelines are used as a way of recognizing when poor choices have been made. *Ifá* teaches that only through effective self-evaluation can real growth occur.

B. *OBATALA ONITOJU AṢẸ* — The Spirit of the Chief of White Cloth as the Source of Counsciousness

Ifá cosmology is based on the belief that the Primal Source of Creation is a form of Spiritual Essence called "*aṣẹ*." There is no literal translation for ase, although it is used in prayer to mean "May it be so."

Ifá teaches that the visible universe is generated by two dynamic forces. One is the force of "*inàlo*," which means "expansion," and the other is the force of "*isokì*," which means "contraction." The first initial manifestation of these forces is through "*ìmo*," which means "light," and through "*aimoyé*," which means "darkness." In *Ifá* myth expansion and light are frequently identified with Male Spirits called "*Orisha'ko*." Contraction and darkness are frequently identified with Female Spirits called "*Orisha'bo*." Neither manifestation of *aṣẹ* is considered superior to the other, and both are viewed as essential elements in the overall balance of Nature.

In *Ifá* cosmology both *ìmo* and *aimoyé* arise from the matrix of the invisible universe which is called "*Imole*," which means "House of Light." Within the house of light there is an invisible substance that transforms spiritual potential into physical reality. The invisible substance that moves between these two dimensions is called *aṣẹ*, and it is *Obatala* who brings the *aṣẹ* of Light into the world.

In his role as Creator of the substance of the universe, *Obatala* is called "*Oloono Ọ̀run*," which means "Owner of that which emerges from the Invisible Realm." Science teaches that energy in the universe creates radiation, and that radiation forms a spectrum of vibrations called light waves. The visible spectrum of light is only a small fragment of the light spectrum. This suggests that the majority of Forces that exist in Creation are invisible to the human eye. Some of these Forces guide the structure of atoms, and some of these Forces guide the structure of galaxies. To call *Obatala Oloono Ọ̀run* is to say that *Obatala* is the Source of all those visible and invisible Forces that generate the physical universe.

III.

ÒNA OBATALA
THE ROADS OF THE SPIRIT OF THE CHIEF
OF WHITE CLOTH

The question of identifying the roads, or aspects of *Obatala* is complex because the *Ifá* concept of *Obatala* embraces a wide spectrum of Spiritual Forces that are referred to as *Orisha 'funfun*. The word "*Orisha 'funfun*" means "Consciousness guided by White- ness." Here the word whiteness is used as a symbol of spiritual elevation and purity. Spiritual elevation refers to the process of projecting consciousness into the future by transcending the limita- tions of the present.

Funfun stands in contrast to the *Ifá* concept of "*dudu*," which means "blackness." There is no negative connotation to the word "*dudu*." In a spiritual context it is a reference to the process of projecting consciousness into the past. It is a reference to the ability of Spiritual Forces to remove the veil of mystery that surrounds the Source of Creation. In *Ifá* the word *dudu*, or blackness, is used as a reference to deep wisdom. It is a word of respect and reverence.

Within the spectrum of Spiritual Forces that come under the general heading of *Orisha 'funfun* there are close to a hundred praise names for the various manifestations of White Cloth that are considered aspects of *Obatala*. These various praise names shift in meaning and significance throughout different regions within the Yoruba Federation.

The simplest way to approach this complex subject is to understand that *Obatala* is frequently referred to as "He." However, the *awo* (mystery) of *Obatala* clearly represents *Obatala* as an androgynous Spiritual Force. Because *Ifá* is based on the under-

standing of Creation as the polarity between powers of expansion
and powers of contraction, the representation of *Obatala* as androgynous suggests that the Power of White Cloth embraces both
forms of primal force in the universe. This idea is consistent with
the science of physics which teaches that light waves form both
particles and waves. A particle is a unit of light which is moving
in on its source, while a wave is a particle of light which is moving
away from its source. These two forms of movement can be
described as expansion and contraction.

When *Obatala* is referred to as the androgynous source of
both forms of light the term "*Orisanla*" is most commonly used.
The word *Orisanla* translates to mean "Source of Consciousness
that is formed by White Cloth." The male, or expansive aspect of
this *Orisha* is most commonly called either "*Obatala*," meaning
"Chief of White Cloth," or "*Obanla*," meaning "Chief of Consciousness that is formed by White Cloth." The female or contractive aspect of this *Orisha* is most commonly called either, "*Iyemowo*,"
which means "Mother of My Hands," or "*Oduduwa*," which means
"Womb that generates Character."

The term *Iyemowo* is generally used in *Ifá* scripture to
describe the Wife of *Obatala*. In symbolic terms the praise name
"Mother of My Hands" is a reference to the ability of the hands to
take care of a persons personal or inner needs. *Ifá* scripture makes
frequent reference to the need for the hands and feet to work
together. This is a proverbial reference to the fact that feet take us
out into the world, which gives them an expansive quality. Our
hands can be used to accommodate personal needs, which is a
contractive quality.

In some regions of Nigeria, *Oduduwa* is considered the male
founder of the Yoruba Nation. In other regions *Oduduwa* is considered the female aspect of *Orisha 'funfun*. The praise name "Womb
that generates Character" is a reference to the ability of White
Cloth, or consciousness, to manifest in a wide range of personal
expressions. It is a symbolic reference to the ability of consciousness to form paradigms of self-understanding that are unique to
itself.

Some of the more common praise names for *Orisha 'funfun* are as follows:

1. *Orisanla* — Consciousness of White Cloth
2. *Obatala* — Chief of White Cloth
3. *Iyẹmowo* — Mother of My Hand
4. *Oduduwa* — Womb that divides Character
5. *Obaorisha* — Chief of the Forces of Consciousness.
6. *Iyemoo* — Our Mother (shortened version of *Iyẹmowo*)
7. *Oba Igbo* — Chief of the Forest
8. *Olu Igbo* — Owner of the Forest
9. *Orisha Olufon* — The First Manifestation of White Cloth
10. *Orishala* — Consciousness of the White Cloth
11. *Orishala Oseremagbo* — Consciousness of the White Cloth which brings us the good things of the Forest
12. *Olofin* — Owner of the Whiteness Which comes from the Sun

These translations of the praise names are approximations of the literal meanings. Because Yoruba language makes extensive use of contractions and eleysions it is often difficult to ascertain with certainty the original root meaning of the words that form a given name. Within the liturgical language of *Ifá* it is common to form words from phrases of praise which are called "*Oriki.*" The word *Oriki* means "Praising the Consciousness." Frequently the *Oriki* which are used as the basis for the praise names of *Orisha* make use of words called "*afoṣẹ*," which have no literal translation. They are words that are designed to resonate with the vibrational power of *Orisha* and have no common use in conversational Yoruba. This aspect of *Ifá* is at the foundation of that aspect of the tradition which remains limited to oral instruction.

IV.

ILÉ ORISHA
THE SHRINE OF THE SPIRIT OF THE CHIEF
OF WHITE CLOTH

A. *ILÉ ORISHA ADURA* — Shrine for Prayer and Meditation
to the Spirit of the Chief of White Cloth

Those who are interested in honoring *Obatala* who have no
access to either *Ifá* or *Orisha* elders can set up a shrine that may
be used for meditation and prayer. The shrine can be used as a focal
point for meditation that can lead to a deeper awareness, appreciation and understanding of *Obatala's* role and function within
Nature. Such a shrine should be set up in a clean place and make
use of white cloth as a setting for other symbolic altar pieces.

Obatala is associated with White Cloth, which is a symbol for
consciousness and consciousness is associated in *Ifá* with "the
breath of life." It is the breath of life and the light of consciousness
that brings us closer to those Spiritual Forces which guide us
towards spiritual transformation and growth. In *Ifá* scripture,
spiritual transformation and growth are symbolized by mountains.
Consequently, *Obatala* has come to be associated with high places.
A shrine to *Obatala* could make use of pictures of sacred mountains, which have the same spiritual function in most cultures
throughout the world.

Obatala is also associated with several animals. The chameleon, the snail, the elephant and the boa constrictor are all considered sacred allies of *Obatala*. Either pictures or sculptures of any
of these animals would enhance the connection with the essence
of *Obatala*.

The shrine should be a place where it is possible to find what *Ifá* calls "*ori tutu*," which means "cool head." This term is a reference to the state of calmness and inner peace that can come through quiet meditation.

B. *ILÉ ORISHA ORIKI* — Shrine for Invocation to the Spirit of the Chief of White Cloth

Shrines which are used for the invocation of *Obatala* are constructed from consecrated religious elements that are presented to a devotee during initiation. These objects may vary, but they generally include a pot that contains the sacred power objects that attract the *aşę* (spiritual essence) of *Obatala*, an *ajija* (pewter bell), a white horse tail fan, a *şękerę* (beaded rattle), *Irin Orisha* (ivory), *Opa Osooro* (metal walking stick), *agba* (sacred drum of *Obatala*) and *sęssęfun* (a white beard).

The *Ifá* calender is based on a five day week and those who have received the *aşę* of *Orisha* generally greet their shrine each morning and say invocations to their shrine every five days. The invocations are called "*Oriki*," which means "praising the consciousness." An example of *Oriki Obatala* is as follows:

> *Ìbà Obatala,*
>> Praise to the Chief of White Cloth,
> *Ìbà Oba Igbo,*
>> Praise to the Chief of the Sacred Grove,
> *Ìbà Oba, N'le ifon,*
>> Praise to the Chief of the Invisible Realm,
> *O fi koko ala rumo.*
>> I salute the Owner of White Cloth.
> *Orisha ni ma sin.*
>> It is the Owner of Consciousness that I serve.
> *Orisha ni ma sin.*
>> It is the Owner of Consciousness that I serve.
> *Orisha ni ma sin.*
>> It is the Owner of Consciousness that I serve.

Obatala o su n'nu ala.
> Chief of White Cloth sleeps in White.

Obatala o ji n'nu ala.
> Chief of White Cloth awakes in White.

Obatala o tinu ala dide.
> Chief of White Cloth gets up in White.

A-di-ni boit ri, mo juba.
> He who creates at will, I thank you.

Aṣẹ.
> May it be so.

C. ADIMU OBATALA — Offerings to the Spirit of the Chief of White Cloth

In all forms of *Ifá* and *Orisha* worship it is traditional to make an offering whenever guidance or assistance is requested from Spiritual Forces. *Adimu* is a term that is generally used to refer to food and drink that is presented to the Spirit of a particular shrine. The idea behind the process of making an offering is that it would be unfair to ask for something for nothing. Those who have an unconsecrated shrine to *Obatala* can make the offering in their own words. Those who have a consecrated shrine to *Obatala* may use the *Oriki* for *Obatala* when making a presentation of *Adimu*. This is usually done when a prayer requesting assistance from *Obatala* is made. The answer to the prayer can then come through divination.

The traditional forms of adimu offered to *Obatala* include:

1. *Omi tutu* — cool water
2. *Iyan* — white sweet potato
3. *Eko* — corn mush
4. *Eyin* — eggs or egg whites
5. *Sinkafa* — rice

Most *Orisha* have some form of alcoholic beverage that is used as *adimu*. As *Obatala's* function is as a role model for ethical behavior and as the Source of clear thinking, there is a taboo against giving alcohol to *Obatala*. This taboo generally applies to those who worship *Obatala* and applies to all those who are initiated into *Obatala's* mysteries.

D. *EBO OBATALA* — Life Force Offerings to the Spirit of the Chief of White Cloth

There is a wide range of ritual procedure in Africa involving the worship of *Orisha*. Many of the differences in ceremonial process reflect regional differences in emphasis rather than essence. In *Ilé Ifẹ́* those who worship *Obatala* tend to make extensive use of *adimu* while making few if any life force offerings directly to the power objects in *Obatala's* shrine. Those regions that do make offerings to *Obatala* generally use either white hens or white pigeons, and snails.

The term "life force offering" is used in reference to the fact that many *Orisha* rituals require preparation of a feast or communal meal. Whenever this occurs the blood from the animal that is used for the meal is given to *Orisha* as an offering. This offering is considered a reaffirmation between *Ikole Orun* (The Realm of the Ancestors) and *Ikole Aye* (Earth). This covenant is an agreement between Spirit and humans that Spirit will provide food for the nourishment of people on earth. In return, the worshipers of *Ifá* and *Orisha* agree to respect the spirit of the animal who provided the food and agree to elevate the spirit of that animal so it will return to provide food for future generations.

Whenever a life force offering is made to any of the *Orisha*, an invocation is generally made to *Ògún* as part of the process. This is a grossly misunderstood aspect of *Ifá* and *Orisha* worship which has suffered from negative stereotypes in the media. It is part of *awo Ògún* (Mystery of the Spirit of Iron) to learn the inner secrets of making life force offerings. When an *Orisha* initiate is making a life force offering it should include an invocation for the *Odu Ogunda*. If the initiate is using the *Lucumí* system of *Mer indinlogun*, the invocation would be to *Ogunda Meji*. In *Ifá* the invocation for life force offerings is to *Ogunda-Irẹtẹ*.

E. *ÌWẸ OBATALA* — Cleansing for the Spirit of the Chief of White Cloth

Ifá and *Orisha* makes extensive use of a wide range of cleansing rituals that are designed to clear away the negative effects of illness, sorrow, grief, anger and contamination by negative spiritual influences. The most fundamental form of cleansings takes the form of empowering water. This means that the water is charged with the power of prayer to accomplish a specific purpose. Once the water has been blessed it can be used to wash specific parts of the body such as the head, the hands or the feet, or it can be used for bathing.

Those who are uninitiated may say a prayer to *Obatala* in their own language and breathe the prayer into the water. The healing effect of the water can be enhanced by adding either coconut milk, snail juice or powdered milk.

Those who are initiated may add their *aşẹ* to the water with the following prayer:

> *Ìbà şẹ Obatala, mo juba.*
>> I praise the Spirit of the Chief of White Cloth and give respect.
>
> *Ìbà şẹ omi tutu, mo juba.*
>> I praise the cool water and give respect.
>
> *Mo ni* (your name)
>> I am (your name)
>
> *Omi tutu, mo be yin,*
>> Cool water, I beg you,
>
> *Fun mi ni alafia.*
>> Bring me peace.
>
> *Fun mi ni ilera.*
>> Bring me a stable home.
>
> *Fun mi ni ori 're.*
>> Bring me the blessings of wisdom.
>
> *Fun mi ni ori tutu.*
>> Bring me the blessing of calmness.

Mo ti dę ìwa-pèlé.

I am a person of good character.

Obatala a ji ala, mo dupe.

I thank the Spirit of the Chief of White Cloth for bringing the blessing of purity.

Aşę.

May it be so.

IRUKERE, Obatala's horse tail staff.

V.

ORISHA 'GUN
THE SPIRIT OF THE CHIEF OF WHITE CLOTH
AND THE MEANING OF SPIRIT POSSESSION

Those who practice the religion of *Ifá* in Africa are generally members of a society that worships a single *Orisha*. These societies are usually refered to by the term "*ègbè*," which means "heart," as in the expression "the heart of the matter." Those who worship *Obatala* would be members of *Ègbè Obatala*. There are regional differences in the use of this term. In some areas societies of *Obatala* worship might be called either "*Ile Obatala*," meaning "House of *Obatala*," or "*Awon Obatala*," meaning "Those who worship *Obatala*."

Regardless of the name used, each of these societies preserves the oral history, myth and wisdom associated with *Awo Obatala* (The Mystery of the Chief of White Cloth). Part of the wisdom that is preserved concerns the discipline used to access altered states of consciousness. Western literature on *Orisha* tends to refer to these states as "possession." This term is inadequate to describe the various forms of trance that are used to assist the *Orisha* worshiper in their understanding of the Mysteries of Being.

Ifá teaches that it is possible to access both *Orisha* (Forces in Nature) and *Egun* (ancestors) through the disciplined use of dreams. The word "*ala*" is used in Yoruba to mean "dream." *Ala* is the last part of the word *Obatala*, and it suggests that the dream state is closely associated with the source of consciousness itself. The word "*alala*" is the word for "dreamer." Because dreamer has a positive connotation in *Ifá*, the word *alala* is a reference to those who are able to make effective use of dreams. *Alala* appears to be a contraction of *ala* and *ala*. In Yoruba, words are often repeated for emphasis or to establish relative relationships. To use the word *ala* twice suggests that the reference to dreamer is an expression of the belief that dreams can access the true source of inner thoughts.

Ifá teaches that it is possible to develop an ongoing relationship with *Orisha* that makes a person sensitive to the influence of *Orisha* on daily effects in their immediate environment. In Western culture this is usually referred to as highly developed intuition. The Yoruba word for intuition is *"ogbon inu,"* which translates literally to mean "the stomach of the earth." *Ifá* metaphysics is based on the idea that those Forces in Nature that sustain life on earth establish certain guidelines for living in harmony with Creation. The development of a sensitivity to these forces is part of the discipline of *Orisha* worship, and this sensitivity is called *ogbon inu*.

There are a number of words that are used to describe those altered states that are commonly referred to as possession. In conjunction with *Orisha* the word *"jogun,"* meaning either "I possess," or "I have" is used to describe a close spiritual connection with Spirit. The phrase *"Orisha'gun,"* is used to describe those who have assumed the characteristics of a particular *Orisha*.

The more common term for possession is *"ini."* This word reveals the *Ifá* perspective on those trance states represent a deep connection with the *aşę* (power) of *Orisha*. The word *ini* appears to be a contraction of *"i,"* which is a personal pronoun, and *"ni"* which is the verb "to be." To use the phrase "I am" as a reference to possession suggests that what is frequently thought of as an intrusion from outside forces is more accurately understood as a process of unlocking the *awo* (mystery) of the inner self. *Ifá* teaches that every person comes to Earth with a spark of divinity at the foundation of their *orí* (inner spirit). Part of the discipline of *Orisha* worship is to access this spark of divinity. This is generally accomplished through initiation, which is designed to guide the initiate towards access to the inner self, which in turn forms a transcendant link with that *Orisha* which is closest to the consciousness of the initiate.

Those who have been through initiation for *Obatala* can enhance their access to *ini* at the same time that offerings are made to their shrine on a five day cycle. This is done by saying *Oriki Obatala* in front of the initiate's *Obatala* shrine. When the *Oriki* is spoken, a candle is lit near the *Orisha* pot and a glass of water is placed near the candle. After the *Oriki* has been completed, the initiate breathes into the glass of water and says the word "*to*," which means "enough." The word to is used at the end of *Oriki* as a seal, or lock to attach the invocation to whatever it is spoken onto.

Using the index finger, the ring finger and the little finger on the left hand, the initiate dips the fingers in the water and runs the water from between the forehead across the top of the head and down the back of the neck. When the fingers are between the eyebrows say, "*iwaju*," which is the name of the power center at the forehead. When the fingers are on the top of the head say, "*ori*," which is the name of the power center at the crown of the skull. When the fingers are on the back of the neck say, "*ipako*," which is the name of the power center at the base of the skull.

A sample of the type of *Oriki* that is used for this process is as follows:

> *Ìbà şę Obatala o rin n'eru ojikutu s'eru.*
>> I respect the Chief of White Cloth who does not fear death.
>
> *Oba n'lé Ifon alabalaşę oba patapat n'ile iranję.*
>> Father of the Realm of the Ancestors is the one who rules all future generations.
>
> *Obatala, Oba igbo oluwaiyę rę e o kę bi owu la.*
>> Chief of White Cloth, Chief of the Sacred Grove, Owner of all blessings, increase my wisdom.
>
> *Obatala o pę o.*
>> Chief of White Cloth I am calling you.
>
> *Obatala o pę o.*
>> Chief of White Cloth I am calling you.
>
> *Obatala o pę o.*
>> Chief of White Cloth I am calling you.

Obatala o pęlę o.
>Chief of the White Cloth I am greeting you.
Obatala ro.
>Chief of the White Cloth descend.
Osun l'ala o fi koko ala rumo.
>Protector of the White Cloth I salute you.
Aşę.
>May it be so.

AJIJA, Obatala's bell.

VI.

ORIN OBATALA
SONG FOR THE SPIRIT OF THE CHIEF OF WHITE CLOTH

Call: *Baba Oba i to aşę to'mole aşę to'mole.*
   Father, the chief has the power to bring the light, to bring the light.
Response: *Oba i to aşę to'mole aşę to'mole.*
   The Chief has the power to bring the light, to bring the light.
Call: *Oba i to aşę to'mole Obatala to'mole.*
   The Chief has the power to bring the light, the Chief of White Cloth
   brings the light.
Response: *Oba i to aşę to'mole aşę to'mole.*
   The Chief has the power to bring the light, the power to bring the
   light.

New Revised

The Master Book of Candle Burning

How to Burn Candles for Every Purpose

POWERFUL PSALM RITUALS

HENRI GAMACHE

Item# 043
$9.95

"How can I burn candles in a manner which will bring me the most satisfaction and consolation?"

In order to answer that question it is necessary to eliminate all technical, dry and often times torturous historical background. It is necessary to sift and sort every fact, scrutinize every detail, search for the kernel.

It is to be hoped that this volume answers that question in a manner which is satisfactory to the reader. It has been necessary, of course, to include some historical data and other anthropological data in order to better illustrate the symbolism involved in modern candle burning as practiced by so many people today.

This data has been accumulated from many sources: it has been culled from literally hundreds of books and articles. The modern rituals outlined here are based upon practices which have been described by mediums, spiritual advisors, evangelists, religious interpreters and others who should be in a position to know.

It has been the author's desire to interpret and explain the basic symbolism involved in a few typical exercises so that the reader may recognize this symbolism and proceed to develop his own symbolism in accordance with the great beauty and highest ethics of the Art.

ISBN 0-942272-56-0 5½"x 8½" $9.95

ITEM #172
$9.95

HELPING YOURSELF WITH
MAGICKAL OILS A-Z

BY MARIA SOLOMON

The most thorough and comprehensive
workbook available on the

**Magickal Powers of
Over 1000 Oils!**

Easy to follow step-by-step instructions
*for more than 1500
Spells, Recipes and Rituals for*
Love, Money, Luck, Protection
and much more!

ISBN 0-942272-49-8 5½"x 8½" $9.95

ITEM #224
$6.95

Revised and Expanded

Success and Power Through Psalms

By Donna Rose

For thousands of years, men and women have found in the Psalms the perfect prayer book, possessing wisdom applicable to every human situation. Wise men and women of deep mystical insight have also learned to decipher the magical formulas David and the other Psalmists hid behind the written words. These formulas help the seeker solve everyday problems, achieve higher states of consciousness, gain material and spiritual wealth, as well as help defend himself or herself against psychic attacks and all manner of dangers.

The Revised and Expanded edition of Donna Rose's classic offers over 300 simple to perform magical rituals to help you manifest all of your desires using the magical powers of the psalms.

ISBN 0-942272-79-X 5½"x 8½ $6.95